i explore

W9-AXP-407

ROCKS

make believe ideas

WHAT'S INSIDE?

Discover more about the amazing world of rocks!

Earth

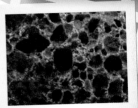
Igneous rocks

Fossils

Minerals

Volcanoes

Sedimentary rocks

Metamorphic rocks

Amazing rocks

Rocks and us

EARTH

Our planet is made of rock. Rock is a hard material made up of minerals. There are three types of rocks – igneous, sedimentary, and metamorphic.

🏠 | i fact | 🔍

ⓘ Earth's hard, outer layer is called the crust. It is made up of sections of rock called tectonic plates.

Meteorites are rocks from outer space that land on our planet. They burn up and become smaller as they fall through the sky, but larger meteorites can create huge craters!

Meteorite

Meteorite crater

crust

inner core

outer core

mantle

i learn

Inside Earth there are layers of very hot rock and metal. The mantle is made of molten rock called magma. Metal makes up the core: the outer core is molten but the inner core is solid because it is crushed so much by all the weight around it.

MINERALS

All rocks are made of minerals. There are thousands of different types of minerals, including gold and amethyst. Most minerals come in regular, block-like shapes called crystals.

---

i fact

Gold is usually found in tiny amounts throughout a larger rock. In 1 tonne of rock, there may only be .04 oz (1 g) of gold!

Gold fragments in quartz

Mining for gold ⊗

8

To identify a mineral, we measure its hardness, or how easy it is to scratch. A mineral's hardness is measured on the Mohs scale, which goes from 1 (softest) to 10 (hardest).

quartz crystal

	Talc	1
	Gypsum	2
	Calcite	3
	Fluorite	4
	Apatite	5
	Feldspar	6
	Quartz	7
	Topaz	8
	Corundum	9
	Diamond	10

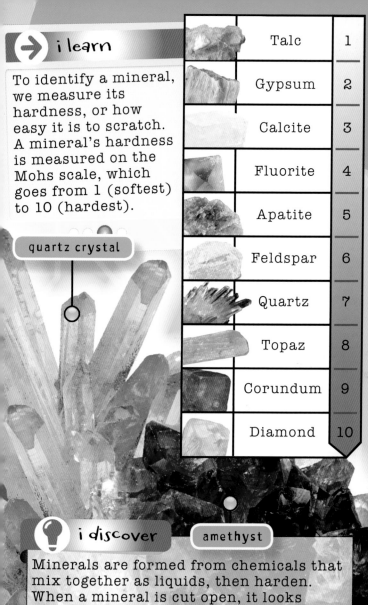

i discover

amethyst

Minerals are formed from chemicals that mix together as liquids, then harden. When a mineral is cut open, it looks the same all the way through.

VOLCANOES

Volcanoes form over weak points in the Earth's crust. Magma flows up from the mantle and bursts through the crust to form new rock. The magma that reaches the surface is called lava.

i learn

Many volcanoes form under the sea where the crust is thin and the mantle is very hot. Lava cools quickly under water, and builds up in layers to form islands.

Volcanic island

Layers of lava

ⓘ Volcanoes that often erupt, such as Mount Etna in Sicily, are called active volcanoes.

Mount Vesuvius

Pompeii

💡 **i discover**

In AD 79, volcanic ash and burning rocks burst out of Mount Vesuvius and almost completely buried the nearby town of Pompeii. The town was only rediscovered 1,700 years later!

volcano

IGNEOUS ROCKS

The word igneous means fiery, and describes rocks made by heat. Igneous rocks form in two ways, creating either intrusive or extrusive igneous rocks.

i fact

i Obsidian, a smooth, glassy rock, forms when lava cools quickly in the air. It is very brittle and when broken it has extremely sharp edges.

Obsidian

When magma is pushed up into the crust and cools, it forms intrusive igneous rocks, such as granite. Extrusive igneous rocks form from lava that bursts out of volcanoes. Pumice forms when lava bubbles into water or air. It is the only rock that floats!

Pumice

Some igneous rocks, such as tuff, form from tiny pieces of rocks and minerals that burst out of a volcano as volcanic ash.

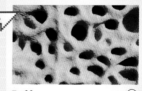

Tuff

i fact

The Giant's Causeway in Ireland is made up of around 40,000 basalt columns formed in a volcanic eruption around 60 million years ago. Basalt is Earth's most common igneous rock.

i explore

SEDIMENTARY ROCKS

Sedimentary rocks are made from small pieces of rock, and often dead plants and animals, which settle at the bottom of areas of water and are crushed together to form new rock.

red sandstone in Arizona, USA

i learn

Sedimentary rocks form in layers. When lakes or seas dry up, we see the layers of sedimentary rock that are left behind.

16

Limestone is a common sedimentary rock that has been used in building for thousands of years. Even the pyramids in Egypt were built with it!

Limestone pyramid

layers

Cliff eroded into an arch by waves

i discover

Wind and water wear away rock. You can see this where waves have worn away rocky cliffs to form arches. This is called erosion. Rock pieces break off and settle together to form new sedimentary rock.

Stalactites

Stalagmites

Stalactites form over thousands of years from the minerals in dripping water. They look like icicles of rock. Stalagmites grow from the ground in the same way.

METAMORPHIC ROCKS

The word metamorphic means to change form. Metamorphic rocks are igneous or sedimentary rocks that have been heated or crushed to produce new rocks.

i learn ✕

Where plates meet, they can pull apart, allowing magma to flow past, or they can crush together. Limestone can be crushed or heated in this way to form the metamorphic rock called marble.

marble

i discover

Metamorphic rocks are also created by meteorites. When a meteorite hits the ground, the force of its landing squashes the nearby rock so much that it becomes metamorphic rock.

Meteorite crater

limestone

Slate tiles

i facts

i Slate is a metamorphic rock that can split into thin layers. This makes it a useful material for building.

Metamorphic rocks are always made of rocks that already exist.

21

FOSSILS

Fossils are the remains of dead plants or animals that have been preserved in rock for millions of years. They are usually found in sedimentary rock.

sedimentary rock

Dragonfly in amber

🏠 | i fact | 🔍

Plants and animals can also be fossilized in tree sap, which turns into see-through amber over many years.

💡 i discover

Fossils teach us about things that lived millions of years ago. We have discovered fossils of feathered dinosaurs, and early dinosaur-like birds such as Archaeopteryx, that show us they are ancestors of today's birds.

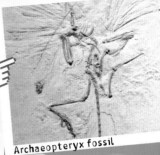

Archaeopteryx fossil

➡️ i learn

Dead animals or plants break down over time, so when a fossil is found, often only an imprint remains. Bones take longer to break down, so we still find skeletons from millions of years ago.

fossil

Prehistoric fossils

AMAZING ROCKS

Rocks shape the landscape around us, and make our world a beautiful and interesting place to live.

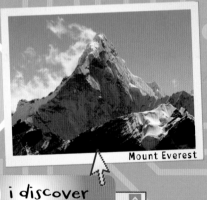

Mount Everest

i discover

Mount Everest is the highest mountain in the world. It is part of a mountain range called the Himalayas.

Columns of tufa rock

When water dries up in salt lakes, the minerals left behind can form columns of tufa rock.

A hoodoo is a column of rock. It has a soft sedimentary base that is eroding away and a hard, igneous top.

igneous top

sedimentary base

Hoodoos in Turkey

The Grand Canyon in America has been carved out over millions of years by the Colorado River. The rock we see at the bottom of the canyon could be as much as 1,840 million years old.

ROCKS AND US

diamond

Over 4,000 years ago, the tools people made from rocks helped them to stay alive. Today, we still use rocks for all kinds of things.

Coal

i discover

Coal is a sedimentary rock that burns very well. It is made from squashed layers of plant material. Burning coal releases energy, which we can use to make electricity.

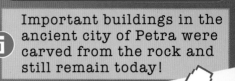

Important buildings in the ancient city of Petra were carved from the rock and still remain today!

ruby

Ancient city of Petra

→ **i learn** ⊗

Diamond is the hardest substance on Earth, so it is used in powerful cutting tools. It also makes valuable jewelry, because it can be polished and smoothed.

Rough diamonds ⊗

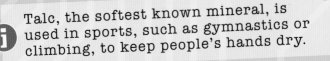

i explore FACTS

i Talc, the softest known mineral, is used in sports, such as gymnastics or climbing, to keep people's hands dry.

Although diamond and graphite are made from the same material, diamond is very hard, but graphite is used in pencils because it is so soft.

The layers in sedimentary rock are called strata.

Anthracite is a metamorphic rock that began as coal but burns more efficiently.

Stonehenge is an amazing rock formation built by humans thousands of years ago!

Igneous rocks erode and collect under the sea to form sedimentary rocks. If they are then heated or crushed, they form metamorphic rocks. This continual change is called the Rock Cycle.